Prais

Living Poems: From ~~~~~~~~~~~~~~~~~

"Linda's poems are a joy to read! Her writings are God-honoring, refreshing, honest, devotional, and filled with truth about God's unconditional love. I believe everyone who reads this will be encouraged and uplifted!"

Pastor Erich Siemens
Calvary Chapel of the Springs
San Marcos, Texas

"The Eyes of My Father causes you to visualize a daily personal relationship with Jesus, while Count Your Blessings is a reminder to be thankful for what God has done in our personal lives. Press On! Encourages the believer to persevere in doing God's will for their lives and The Prayer of a Grandmother's Heart is a perfect prayer for any grandparent praying over a grandchild going through troublesome times. Each one of these poems, mentioned above, is very descriptive and based on one's relationship with Jesus Christ."

Jody Everett
Bachelor of Science in Electrical
Engineering (BSEE) & Design Engineer
Austin, Texas

Living Poems:

From the Father's Heart
Inspirational poems

Living Poems:
From the Father's Heart
Inspirational poems

Author: Linda Delgado

Editor: Michael Goins

This book is dedicated to my Heavenly Father, who so graciously brought it into existence. This book would not exist without His inspiration.

TABLE OF CONTENTS

Table of Figures

ACKNOWLEDGMENTS

I'm so thankful to the Lord for all the people He used in bringing this book together. It's been such a blessing to have so many brothers and sisters in the *Family of God,* many of which were instrumental in encouraging me to pursue writing as a gift from the Lord.

Robie Nagai, was one of my *sisters* that has become a very good friend of mine. Since the first day I met her, I saw she had such an open heart for the Lord. She encouraged me to pursue *writing* even further. At the time I was posting encouraging words on social media. I would write (whatever the Lord put on my heart) and entitled them *Matters from the Heart.*

Soon after that, I told my cousin, Michael Goins, about the encouragement Robie had been giving me, in pursuing writing He immediately thought it was a great idea and said he would love to see my manuscript, when it was ready. He also said, that if it was good enough, he would assist me in getting it published. Once he said this, I knew that I was following God's will. I could see how things were all starting to fall into place. At the same time, he volunteered to be my editor! Sunday afternoons (on Zoom), from 4pm – 4:45pm CDT, became our meeting time for brainstorming and revising the poetry book. At that time, the "final product", was directed more for the prison ministry, which he was a part of (TPPM- Transformation Project Prison Ministry).

During this time, I unknowingly had prior experience through my mother. My Aunt Jeanette sent me a picture via text message (on my phone). She told me she found a piece of paper in an old cabinet my mother kept in her bathroom. It was a poem she had written entitled, "Youth". My aunt explained to me the story of this poem came to be. My mother had written this, when she was still able to sit up in a chair. This became another step into my newfound journey. To me, this was the Lord confirming what I was already doing. Writing for Him. I never knew my mother had written poetry in her last days. What a precious memory!

Another thing that had come to mind as well, was about a month before that, a fellow writer asked me if I had tried *free form* poetry. I said I was willing to try it. Then when I saw my mother's poem, it was in *free form* poetry! Now I had an example of how to write it. I am so blessed to know that my mother did this earlier in my life, with no knowledge of how God would use this for His glory!

I also want to give a special thank you to my brother, Larry Garrett, for playing a big part in encouraging me to continue writing. After finding out he had bone cancer, I called every day to talk to him. I didn't want to miss any more time than I already had. When he had read a couple of the poems, I never expected the phone call I received. He had no idea that I needed to hear the words he was about to tell me. He encouraged me to continue writing! He had no idea of the impact his words would make on me. I later found out, that he held on to those two poems, every night until his last day.

I believe I need to let my husband, Rodolfo (Rudy) Delgado, know how much I appreciate his understanding, patience, love, and continued support, at the beginning, during, and while putting the book together, as well as writing in general.

On a more somber note: Unfortunately, Michael Goins did not get to see the book to the finish. It was tragic news to learn of the car accident he was in March 23, 2022. I know I will see him again, in Heaven someday, but until then I will continue to pursue writing for the Lord, for His glory. He will be sorely missed, as he touched everyone he encountered. He was a strong pillar of wisdom, as well and I was fortunate to have him help me with the editing of this book. Even though we were cousins, he was just like a brother to me. His compassion for others was contagious. He would give you the shirt off his back, if he felt you needed it. Even people from other states, whom he either worked with or just played online games with, enjoyed his friendship and comradery. Every Saturday, he would email a "newsletter" to family and friends, called *"The Saturday Morning Post."* This was a weekly update of, not just his life, but others, as well. My favorite part of the newsletter was the

"Safari" trips he would take with his two big dogs, Sunny i.e., Sundance and Wulf. On these trips, Mike would take beautiful wildlife pictures and post them in the newsletter (deer's, various types of birds, etc.). Some of the pictures, he has allowed me to use throughout this book. I will especially miss our "business" meetings we had every Sunday afternoon. They were always more than just meetings. This was the closest we got to be with each other. He was very precise in time management. After our time was up, he made it a point to spend time with his wife, Denise. This showed me how much compassion he had for others, especially his wife and family (no matter how near or far they were).

What a beautiful journey this has been for me. Only my Heavenly Father knows where this writing adventure will lead me after this book. I did have some discouraging moments, when I asked the Lord, "Do you really want me to continue writing?" Desperate for an answer amid my discouraged heart. I knew as always; He would let me know in the way He always does. Gently, with love, and understanding, dowsed with His mercy and grace. I did not know that within just a few days, God's confirmation would be there, on time, as always.

PREFACE

Each poem herein is thoughtfully written, reflecting various situations in my life. Every word should guide you to feel the very heartbeat of God. Some of the poems are written with great, heartfelt emotion: from peace and joy, to sadness, hope and faith. These poems paint a beautiful picture of my relationship with my Savior, Mentor, and Friend – Jesus Christ. You may find one poem that depicts what you are going through in your own personal life. Some or all of them will tug at your own heartstrings! Just open yourself to receive whatever the Lord has for you in the reading.

INTRODUCTION

When I was younger, I avoided reading poetry. I would cringe at the very thought of writing it for my English classes. It was too hard to understand! I soon found out that God had other plans regarding poetry! Fictional books were more my forte', because they would leave me on the edge of my seat, eager to find out what was on the next page.

My family and I began a new journey with the Lord after making a big move to San Marcos from Corpus Christi, Texas. At first it was a little rough, but once we established ourselves, things started to work out.

Soon after getting settled into the routine of things, we began looking for a church home, preferably close to our apartment. I had continued attending a Bible study group in one of the area churches (Bible Study Fellowship i.e., BSF) and that was where I met Robie Nagai. During our time of conversing, I began to share how we were looking for a church to go to. She was excited to invite me to Calvary Chapel of the Springs, here in San Marcos! Upon entering the doors, that Sunday morning, Robie and others welcomed us as we came in the church. Before we left, we had met the Pastor, Erich Siemens. Although it was half the size of the church we came from, we felt right at home as we entered the building. It was very evident that this would be our new church home!

Several years later, I had begun writing, not knowing what God's plans were for me at the time. It began with just a casual posting on social media, used to uplift and edify the body of Christ. This collection of postings was called "Matters from the Heart." A few months later, I was encouraged to take my writing one step further, into poetry. I began to recognize the Lord's guidance in the poems I had written. Soon after that I found myself writing poetry for the Lord, exclusively.

Most of the poems were written from individual experiences in my own life, as well as the lives of others. I have written summaries, carefully placing them at the beginning of each section and poem. This introduces you to the origin and the inspiration for each one.

So how does all of this qualify me to write poetry now? Until He calls me home, I will follow my Savior, Jesus Christ, wherever He leads me. May the Lord bless you as you venture into His love and presence.

PART ONE: FRIENDSHIP

*. . . I remember you in my prayer's
night and day...being mindful of your
tears, that I may be filled with
joy,*

2 Timothy 1:3-4

Figure 1: Badger Buddies

Poems about friendship are few and far between. The poems in this part speak about our friendship with Jesus. When he dwelt among others, He was known to some as Lord, Master, and Teacher; but the disciples knew Him as the Messiah, the "Son of the Living God!" When Jesus spoke in John 15:15, He wanted every believer there to know, that even though He was/is the Messiah, they will always be regarded as His friends. What compassion is shown here! How awesome to know that the King of Kings, regards us as His friend!

As believers, Jesus walks with us every day. Sometimes, when it gets hard to go on, He is always there to comfort us and hold us, as a compassionate, loving Father would. He gives great hugs! God is a good listener; He keeps every tear. He has a never-ending amount of unconditional love for us!

1. MY LOVE FOR YOU

I am often reminded of the scripture that says: Many will say to Me in that day, 'Lord, Lord, have we not prophesied in Your name, cast out demons in Your name, and done many wonders in Your name?' And then I will declare to them, 'I never knew you; depart from Me, you who practice lawlessness!' (Matthew 7: 22 – 23). In the Amplified version of these same two verses, Jesus says, "I never knew you; Depart from Me [you are banished from My presence], you who act wickedly [disregarding My commands].

Everything we do should be an expression of Christ's love for others. Our love for the Lord should be as limitless as His love for us, though we often get side-tracked with the cares of this life. How much do you love Him?

...For He Himself has said, "I will never leave you nor forsake you."

Hebrews 13:5

My Love for You

My love for You, Lord, will always be true,
You're there with me in whatever I do.

Your friendship to me is like no other,
being as close as my sister or brother.

The love You have for me is forever,
so that we can always be together.

Together, through till the end of time.
Knowing You, Lord, is truly sublime.

Walking with me in each step that I take,
You've shown me more of You, in a great way.

How great, O Lord, is my love for You.
I'll gladly serve you in all that I do.

2. YOUR EVERLASTING LOVE

The unconditional love of God was expressed through His Son, Jesus.

No matter how great our sins, Jesus still forgives us. It's easy to be caught up in the things of this world, but Jesus is always there to pick us up.

As believers, we now have the *Living Water* just as our Lord promised we would. When He is invited into our hearts to reside, His Spirit indwells within us. That's when He can begin to make changes in our life, as we become yielded to Him.

> *He who believes in Me, as the scripture has said, out of his heart will flow rivers of living water.*
>
> ***John 7:38***

Your Everlasting Love

How can I deny Your love for me,
after all You've done to set me free?

Over all the years that have come and gone,
my heart still longs for us to be as One.

How I long to see Your face,
outside of the human race.

Your blood flowing from the cross,
lifts me up when I am lost.

Jesus' sweet Spirit flows deep within,
as a covering for all my sin.

Thank you, Jesus for Your everlasting love,
that is divinely inspired from our Father above.

3. MY FOREVER FRIEND

We all go through tough times and Jesus is aware of every move that's made. The good thing is, not only is He our Savior and Lord, but He is also our "BFF" (*Best Friend Forever*).

What a friend Jesus truly is! He won't abandon us when times get rough and the best part of all. He is walking with us through everything! Do you have a friend who will do *all* these things? Jesus is truly closer than any brother we could ever have.

> *No longer do I call you*
> *servants, for a servant does not*
> *know what His master is doing;*
> *but I have called you friends,*
> *for all things that I heard from*
> *My Father I have made known*
> *to you.*

> **John 15:15**

My Forever Friend

As my tears seem to melt my very soul,
my Master's hands have begun to unfold.

His hands are catching every single tear,
as He is holding me ever so near.

Holding me oh, so closely to His heart,
reminding me He will never depart.

He's the One who can heal me from within,
causing the mending to fin'ly begin.

His name is Jesus, my Savior and Lord.
One day I'll reign with Him forevermore!

The heavenly realm, where time has no end,
as He'll always. be *my Forever Friend*.

PART TWO: THANKFULNESS

Not that I speak in regard to need, for
I have learned in whatever state I am,
to be content:

Philippians 4:11

Figure 2:Fluffed Turkey

Close your eyes and just imagine being in the presence of God, the Father. Begin to bask in His love and peace. When we focus more on the Lord, everything else falls into place at its proper time. We need to practice sitting still before Him, learning to lean on His understanding and not ours.

Sometimes we needlessly stress ourselves out. Just because the answers to our prayers are not visible to us yet, does not mean God's not at work - - He always is!

1. MY BELOVED

In our daily walk with the Lord, we don't *always feel* that He's there with us. Just because we don't *feel* His presence doesn't mean we're alone. Jesus said, "I will never leave you nor forsake you" (Hebrews 13:5). What a blessing it is to have a close friend who will stay with us, no matter what we are going through.

Our Heavenly Father created *"all of creation,"* and He is omnipresent with us. While in His presence, as we surrender more to Him, Christ's blood cleanses us from all our sins.

> *A man who has friends must himself be friendly, But there is a friend who sticks closer than a brother.*
>
> **Proverbs 18:24**

My Beloved

Oh Lord, Most High,
I love dwelling in Your presence!

When I'm with You,
I'm enveloped in Your essence!

I'm so thankful for Your goodness to me,
even when I expect things I cannot yet see.

So, therefore, good things,
come to those who do wait.

The blessings will flow,
when You enter this place.

My faith, hope, and trust,
are entwined in Your love.

Your Holy Word cleanses,
with each drop of Your blood.

2. HIS REFRESHING WORD

God's Words breathe life into everything we see. All His creation has life, whether we see it or not. Ultimately, He has the final word in any situation in our own lives. That final word was sealed, with His heartfelt love, when Jesus said, "It is finished," on the cross.

We take so many things for granted, in life. We need to ask ourselves, before our time has come, are we aware of the price God, the Father, paid so that we could have a chance to have *open, one-on-one* fellowship with our Creator? That *chance* became a reality, when the *curtain* was torn in half, eliminating the "middleman" (the priest), that was separating us from God. Not only was our *free will* expanded, but we no longer had to have a priest contact God for us.

When Jesus breathed His last breath here on earth, our sins (past, present, and future) were forgiven. We now, can have the opportunity to an ultimate, one-on-one relationship with the Creator of the universe. God, our Abba Father, who made it easier to have a one-on-one relationship with our Him.

That same opportunity, which was opened for all, over 2,000 years ago, still stands today.

And the glory which You gave
Me I have given them, that they
may be one just as We are One;

John 17:22

His Refreshing Word

Breathing in all the air around me,
seeing as far as my eyes can see.

The beauty and reality of all God's creation,
takes my breath away as I see its daily ministration.

Breathing in each day that He's given to me,
shows His love in my life and how to be free.

Even when Jesus surrendered His last breath,
they would soon realize He had conquered death.

The unwinding of God's infinite plan,
led to the redemption of every man.

The Lamb was slain, paying the highest price,
exchanging our sin for eternal life.

The fall of man, reversed with His final breath,
was known throughout history to have a great depth.

Jesus, on the cross, overcame the devil's kingdom
and with one final breath He had given us freedom!

The air we now breathe as His believers,
has been restored to many deceivers.

Without lies they'd been taught since youth,
they took a deep breath in the power of truth!

The truth of God's Word is like a breath of fresh air,
the power it contains lifts hearts in despair.

Nothing can compare to His infinite Word,
for once it's breathed in, it begins a new work!

3. MORE OF YOU & LESS OF ME

Our desire should be to serve the Lord, such that we lay our whole day at His feet before we walk out the door. We often take back what we have submitted to Him in the past. The only way that Jesus can lead, is if we yield ourselves to His leadership.

When we surrender ourselves to Jesus, we begin to see, day by day, changes that we've looked forward to. This is when we draw closer to Him, as children of God. With gratitude, our hearts are encouraged, and we become able to share the Good News with others.

...in everything give thanks;
for this is the will of God in
Christ Jesus for you.

I Thessalonians 5:18

More of You & Less of Me

As I stand before You Lord,
I lay it all at Your feet.

Fill me with Your Spirit,
so that others may see.

My heart's desire is to have
more of You and less of me.

Sharing with them Your great love
and how You sent Jesus, Your only Son.

How He was crucified on a cruel tree,
on top of a hill named Old Calvary.

May each day begin and end with You,
bringing me closer in all that I do.

At the end of the day,
as I've followed Your ways,

My life with You,
never will stray.

As I now rest in Your arms,
I know I'm safe from all harm.

I can now feel
Your sweet, gentle peace.

21

4. THE EYES OF MY FATHER

Just imagine yourself standing before the Lord, Himself. As your eyes meet with His, it's as if He can see right through you. There is more to see as *you* see the radiance of not just His majesty, but His everlasting, unconditional love.

Looking into His eyes not only is revealing weak spots in our own lives, but seeing through Jesus, everything He wants me to do, right here, right now!

His Word literally shows me how to please Him, by walking according to what His Word says and living life as, a believer of Jesus Christ.

Oh, the compassion in His eyes, will forever examine my spirit and always tell me what I need to work on, to be even more pleasing to Him.

For the Lord is good; His
Mercy is everlasting, And His
truth endures to all
Generations.

Psalm 100:5

The Eyes of My Father

As I look into my Father's eyes,
I'm absorbed by His presence.
He can see all that I am and will be,
within His very essence.

His eyes seem to go right through me,
while we are standing face-to-face.
His unconditional love for me
and His amazing grace.

The mercy that He's shown to me,
has been so real in my life.
I am pushing forward daily,
while I'm walking through the strife.

How can I lose focus,
on His destiny for me?
When that day finally comes,
His perfection I will be!

5. COUNT YOUR BLESSINGS

How you perceive things that happen in your life (a glass that is half empty or half full) will oftentimes determine what direction it will take. We may not always have what we want in this life, but we need to take an inventory of what we already have. Be grateful for what you have, because your eternal treasures are in Heaven and our Heavenly Father is our provider. He will never let His children go hungry (spiritually or physically).

Sometimes it's hard to be thankful in *all* things, as is suggested in His Word. That's why Paul tells us (I Corinthians 15:31) that we need to *daily die to self* and we're to be *living sacrifices* (Romans 12:1) in our daily walks with the Lord. Doing these things, will help us to be thankful.

What are you thankful for today?

> *I beseech you therefore,*
> *brethren, by the mercies of God,*
> *that you present your bodies a*
> *living sacrifice, holy, acceptable*
> *to God, which is your*
> *reasonable service.*
> **Romans 12:1**

Count Your Blessings

So here it is, that time of year,
when I think back on things, I've held dear.

Different times I'm thankful for,
reflecting on what's no more.

Reminding myself of how far I've come,
before I came to know Jesus, Your Son.

Being reborn into Your Kingdom was a thrill,
now I'm forever indebted to do *Your* will.

My love for Him grew from there,
thankful that my sin He did bear.

Remembering that day; how wonderful I felt;
when I was delivered from the jaws of hell!

All the trials that You've brought me through,
now I know I was lost without You.

I'm thankful for the home I have,
though others may just see a shack.

So thankful for the food I've been given,
that I can continue in giving it.

It's so sad that the world today,

refuses to see things our way.

They're being engulfed in their own desires,
that they've placed their beliefs into the fire!

We need to be thankful for what we don't see,
even when there are times, we may disagree.

There's always something to be thankful for,
think of one before you walk out your door!

PART THREE: IN GOD'S PRESENCE

Therefore, having been justified by faith, we have peace with God through our Lord Jesus Christ, through whom also we have access by faith into this grace in which we stand, and rejoice in hope of the glory of God.

Romans 5:1-2

Figure 3: Dove on a Cross

As we yield to Jesus more and more each day, He fills us with joy, peace, and love. His peace is like no other. In turn, we begin to show compassion to Him and those around us.

We need to keep in mind that it may never be an easy road, but Jesus is always willing and ready to help us. Just saying the name of Jesus can put everything into perspective. Darkness can't survive where light is.

1. HIS GLORIOUS PRESENCE

Being in God's presence gives us an abundant amount of joy, peace, and love. These are just some of the things we will experience when we yield to the Holy Spirit.

We're able to experience joy unspeakable, as He is always present with us. The joy that only the Spirit can bring reveals that we are His.

The *peace that surpasses all understanding* is not anything close to what the world has to offer. His peace is indescribable. Once you experience it you will never want the world's peace again.

> *Now may the God of hope fill you with all joy and peace in believing, that you may abound in hope by the power of the Holy Spirit.*
> **Romans 15:13**

His Glorious Presence

Lord, You are truly the Most High God!
Your presence gives us joy, peace, and love.

Joy that is indescribably great,
more than what we could do or say.

Peace that is beyond what this world can give.
The peace that comes from Your Spirit, within.

Your love Lord, has no boundaries or conditions,
causing our faith to rise with its fruition.

The same love You've given, since our first breath
and You'll still be there with us even past death.

Each day that we live, it is only for You
and to glorify You in all that we do.

2. BEING IN HIS PRESENCE

Once we've focused our whole being on Jesus and all that He stands for, the Holy Spirit opens our hearts and minds. How much greater is our Savior than the problems that we face. Being in His presence is something we wish could last forever! The Good News is that it will last forever!

Experiencing His unconditional love, while He gives us a big hug. All while basking in His presence! In that moment of being near Him, there's a mixture of emotions. The atmosphere changes when we feel the Lord's presence. His Holy Spirit abides in us, and we are filled to overflowing with His love for others and ourselves. It's just a sweet spiritual time with the Lord!

> Do not cast me away from
> Your presence, And do not
> take Your Holy Spirit from
> me. Restore to me the joy of
> Your salvation, And uphold
> me by Your generous Spirit.
>
> ***Psalm 51:11-12***

Being in His Presence

When your presence is near,
I have nothing to fear.

Gazing into Your eyes,
it seems there's no time.

I know that I'm standing in Your presence,
when I'm baptized in Your essence.

Helping me walk through each night,
Your Word shines the way with might.

Your presence so enthralls me Lord,
my spirit keeps absorbing more!

Looking forward to the sweetest peace,
Your arms embracing, all strife ceased.

3. WALKING WITH JESUS

What a privilege, as a child of God, to have an ever-present walk with the Lord. Being able to talk to Him, as our best friend, knowing He is *closer than our brother*. We can trust and share our most intimate feelings with Him. Things we would tell no one else. In turn, we can feel conviction (not guilt) from His Spirit, at the same time. No one is closer than Jesus.

When we're walking with Jesus, on destiny's path, we need to remember He will be with us no matter what our situation is.

> *...For He Himself has said, "I will never leave you or forsake you."*
>
> ### *Hebrews 13:5*

Walking with Jesus

As we're coming to Your Throne, Lord,
standing here in awe,
we're drawn in by Your majesty
and who You are!

Your love is unconditional
and You're always by our side.
Our hands are joined together,
as each given day goes by.

As we look into Your face, Lord,
we can hear You say,
My hand will never leave yours
unless you turn away.

You're always there
with each battle we face.
Your Spirit guides us,
as we see Your face.

This sacrifice You've made,
for all the world to see,
is only understood,
when we have been set free.

4. THE CLEANSING SPIRIT OF GOD

We all have a desire within our hearts to experience the Lord's presence! The best part is, just the mere mention of His name and He is in our midst. If you're a believer in Christ, you've experienced His presence every day!

His cleansing Spirit reveals to us when we have done something wrong.   As we humbly come before Him, we begin to realize how much we truly need Him in our lives. Knowing that He's with us in whatever we may go through, is so comforting. He gives each of us the same love that He does each of His children.

The one thing that the lost souls of this world don't realize is the fact that God will not force them to believe in Him. He willingly gives us that choice! Have you chosen to believe in Him and serve Him till He returns? I pray that you will if you haven't already. Let His Spirit cleanse you from your sin today, won't you?

But if we walk in the light as He is in the light, we have fellowship with one another, and the blood of Jesus Christ His Son cleanses us from all sin.

1 John 1:7

The Cleansing Spirit of God

Father, let Your Spirit rain on me,
cleanse my spirit from all sin and grief.

Refresh me with Your love, so sweet,
as I humbly lay the day at Your feet.

Lord, as I give you my hands, I submit them to You.
Let them bring glory in all that I do.

Following You as I walk in Your ways,
knowing You're with me in each passing day.

Through each day that goes by,
nothing will be hidden from the naked eye.

Every drop of Your Spirit,
guides me in how to get through it.

Basking in Your presence, Lord,
my soul is no longer torn.

Cause the cares of this world to be released,
as Your Spirit rains His sweet peace on me.

5. FOREVER WITH OUR SAVIOR

Every believer has a passionate desire to be in the Lord's presence. This desire continues to grow in us as we receive from His Word daily. The Word of God shares a big piece of Gods heart. Showing how He desires to be with us, nonstop, is just one of the things He shows us.

This poem speaks of our soul's longing to be with our Lord and Savior. The yearning to see our loved ones, "who have been there a while" and to experience the everlasting joy that comes with it.

> *You have made known to me the ways of life; You will make me full of joy in Your presence.*
>
> ***Acts 2:28***

Forever with Our Savior

Longing to see You face-to-face,
kneeling before You, in this place.

My heart is yearning to be with You,
when at last, I'll have a perfect view!

Seeing my loved ones who've been there a while.
Oh, it will be so great to see their smiles!

No more are tears and sadness,
only joy, peace, and gladness.

Yes, my soul does long for that perfect day,
when I'll be with You, forever to stay!

PART FOUR: BROKENNESS

The Lord is near to those who have
a broken heart, And saves such as
have a contrite spirit.

Psalm 34:18

Figure 4: Broken Old House

We often fail because of mistakes we make in this life. When we make mistakes over and over, our heart breaks and we feel there is nothing more we can do. It is at that moment when we need to shift our perspective and look to Jesus for our strength. II Corinthians tells us, ". . .for My strength is made perfect in weakness."

As we come before the Lord asking for His forgiveness, God is drawn to our broken and contrite heart.

1. CONFIRMED SECURITY

Even though the enemy would like us to believe that we are alone in our circumstances, we never are. We need to remind ourselves that Jesus will never turn away from us, especially when we're broken.

Jesus alone can put the pieces of your life back together. He alone can mend the wounds with His love and His grace. He alone showed us His love, when Jesus shed His precious blood for us, so we could freely come to Him with our burdens, laying them all at the foot of the cross.

Are you broken today? Open your heart, won't you? You have nothing to lose, but eternal life, with Jesus to gain.

The sacrifices of God
are a broken spirit, a
broken and a contrite
heart – These, O God,
You will not despise.

Psalm 51:17

Confirmed Security

O Lord, up above,
fill me with Your love!

The enemy told me I'm just a fool
when I spoke scriptures of what's true.

The next thing I knew, I heard God so clear,
as His Spirit spoke to me, "I am here."

It was then, my spirit realized,
a broken heart, He will not despise*.

My Abba Father had heard my cry.
He clearly, had not passed me by!

After He picked me up and dusted me off,
we continued our walk among the lost.

When we were walking, I could hear Him say,
"My child, I've walked with you through every day."

He even followed me when I walked away.
Knowing what I know now, I am here to stay!

So, from my heart to yours I would like to say,
He'll always be with you, no matter what day.

We can *and* are assured,
in Jesus, we're secure.

*Psalm 51:17

2. THE MASTERPIECE

When we're first born, we don't know who Jesus Christ is. As infants we focus on being dependent on our parents. Being that we're born into sin, the dependency even in infancy begins to be manipulative in how we depend on others to get what we want. We grow up thinking and depending on having control of our lives. Even though we seem to have that control, something will always be missing. Someone who should be accepted as the very cornerstone of our lives.

You see, God's Word says that we are created in His image. We were created by Him, for Him, and in Him! He is the Masterpiece/Cornerstone of our lives. Without Him we are incomplete.

For God so loved the world that He gave His only begotten Son, that whoever believes in Him should not perish but have everlasting life.

John 3:16

The Masterpiece

When, at first, I entered this life,
I didn't know what Christ was like.

The world seemed like a puzzle to me,
and there was so much I could not see.

I was searching for that perfect piece,
who could give me joy, beyond belief.

Desiring to find the One,
who gives to all unending love.

Although I knew, in my heart,
Jesus Christ could be that part.

Becoming so overwhelmed with everything,
I never knew *the One* who could set me free.

My destiny still waiting for me,
yet I could not see how that could be.

Then one night, I cried out in desperation,
to the One I knew, who could give me salvation.

It was then my life's puzzle began to make sense,
Jesus was the One piece, that I knew was still left.

So many puzzles were incomplete in my life.
because I lacked the *Master,* who lived and died.

In Him I am now complete,
He is my life's *"Master"* piece.

3. THE SHINING TRUTH

This poem speaks about someone who has passed or strayed away from the Lord. The person who is narrating, is wishing they were here so they could see how God had such great plans for their life.

So often we tend to forget the calming peace that God can give us through His Son, Jesus. His *Truths* can shed light in the darkest shadows of any life. We are each created so uniquely, that none of us are the same, on the outside.

On the inside, however, God has put together such a complex, intertwined, network of nerves, muscles, bones, tendons, etc. Even though we are so complex, He loves us all the same. He has *no* favorites!

I so look forward to the day when we will reign with Him for all eternity! The invitation to do the same is challenging you today. Are there some areas in your life that need Jesus' *Shining Truth* to reveal? Do you know someone that has gone their own way, leaving God behind them?

And the glory which You gave
Me I have given them, that they
may be one just as We are one:

John 17:22

The Shining Truth

Many times, I've wished you were here,
to learn of how God knows your fears.

Fears that have haunted you through the night,
causing slumbering peace to take flight.

Every time you've felt alone,
God has wanted to hold you as His own.

Please don't doubt His love for you,
because this love can make you new!

The devil has lied to you all this time,
desiring only to shatter your mind.

Every detail known to man,
is held in the palm of God's hand.

You see, we're *each* special in a unique way.
God gave us a purpose-filled life for each day.

We each have a place in God's heart,
and He orders our steps until we depart.

Departing for our eternal home,
we will see Jesus on His throne!

Won't you come and join us there,
as He takes away all our cares?

PART FIVE: ENCOURAGEMENT

Let your conduct be without covetousness
be content with such things as you have for
He Himself has said, "I will never leave
you nor forsake You."

Hebrews 13:5

Figure 5: Group of Mule Deer

Have you ever noticed when you need help with something, that your Heavenly Father is always there to encourage you? Jesus is closer than any "brother" you will ever have. He doesn't desert you when times get tough.

You may receive encouragement through a co-worker, a non-believer, a relative, a stranger, or even someone you can't stand to be around! Sometimes we tend to forget exactly how big God is!

1. UNWASTED PRAYERS

No prayers get past our Heavenly Father. He hears every one of them. Especially *the sinner's prayer*! His Son, Jesus, the Savior of the world, is always interceding for us. I honestly believe it's God's love that motivates Him to pray for us as often as He does!

Can you imagine praying for someone non-stop? In I Thessalonians 5:17-18, Paul said we are to *pray without ceasing.* The amplified version of this same scripture gives a little more detail: *be unceasing **and** persistent in prayer...for this is the will of God for you in Christ Jesus.* Let's get a clearer picture of what he meant by *persistent.* Merriam Webster gives this definition (**to persist**): ***To go on resolutely or stubbornly in spite of opposition, importunity, or warning.*** Translated further: To persevere no matter what obstacles may come your way!

As the old cliché would say: *Pick yourself up and dust yourself off and start all over again*! Being "persistent" means that you **keep** going instead of starting all over again. In other words: Pick up where you left off and keep on going! That's what Paul meant by, *pray without ceasing!*

> *The Lord is far from the wicked,*
> *But He hears the prayer of the*
> *righteous.*

> ***Proverbs 15:29***

Unwasted Prayers

'My prayers are not a waste of time!',
says my brain, to this heart of mine.

The Lord above, I know He hears,
and every tear of mine, He holds so dear.

Any doubts I have, they may try to interfere,
but once again, I know He hears!

The enemy will consistently lie,
by telling me repeatedly, that I am wasting my time!

But I know, my Lord, up above, near and far,
He hears me cry out to Him, up through the stars.

His Word speaks of strength, power, and love,
that only can come from the Trinity, the three in one!

I proclaim to you all, that are here in this place,
He does answer prayers, with His powerful grace!

So, to all those that believe prayers are a waste. . .,
only the Lord, above, can give you mercy and grace!

2. HIS PEACE FOR YOUR TIME

It's easy to become so busy with everyday life that we forget the most important One of all. Jesus Christ, our Savior! Without Him we wouldn't have the opportunity to have a one-on-one relationship with God, our heavenly Father.

Unfortunately, much of the world has been looking to blame others for anything and everything. We, ourselves, tend to forget to give God *our* time for *His* peace.

What a better place the world would be, if we would lean on our Lord more and more, instead of putting Him last. His peace is like no other. He *can and will* give you *peace for your time*. Won't you let Him today?

> *and the peace of God, which*
> *surpasses all understanding,*
> *will guard your hearts and*
> *minds through Christ Jesus.*
>
> **Philippians 4:7**

His Peace for Your Time

At the beginning of each God-given day,
it's very easy to be stretched every way.

Becoming unaware of the time,
the day has begun to lose its rhyme.

Worldly thoughts of one another,
has put brother against brother.

We've become so entrapped in our thinking,
we don't realize the poison we're drinking!

Sinking into the world's pitfalls of life,
which causes more trouble – leading to strife.

Rushing around from one place to another,
taking away time to be with our Father.

Jesus is patiently waiting our return,
the very One whom we have so easily burned.

Despite how much we have pushed Him away,
He'll still be there at the end of the day.

He never leaves our side,
through the end of time.

Has your life become a busy disarray?
Come to Jesus, He will give you peace today.

3. THE SWORD OF TRUTH

Our Savior told us we would have trials and tribulation in this world. He also told us to not be dismayed, for He had *overcome the world* (John 16:33). Using our sword (Holy Bible) daily will defeat the enemy on any given day. We know this to be true, because when Jesus was going through the temptation in the wilderness (Matthew 4:1-11), He, Himself quoted words from scripture.

You see, Jesus will not leave us to fend for ourselves. We often hear the cliché' "sink or swim", meaning we either succeed by ourselves for the given task or we don't and wind up making a fool out of ourselves. Jesus isn't like that. He said several times in His Word, He would **never** *leave us or forsake us!* He said this many other places in the Bible, as well. He wants us to succeed in life, but in order to make it through all the trials and tribulations, we must do it *His way.* He has already given us the Armor of God. That's right. He has control over the situation, we don't. He told us we would have trials and tribulation in this world. He also told us to not be dismayed, for He had overcome the world (John 16:33). On any given day we can defeat the enemy, using our Sword. The key to all of this: to trust Him with your heart, mind, and soul!

> *...and the take the...sword of the Spirit, which is the word of God;*
>
> **Ephesians 6:17**

The Sword of Truth

When I'm tired of running this race,
Christ sets me on a different pace.

He slows me down so I can hear,
His Words that I hold, oh so near.

As I'm beginning to recite each one,
the enemy's troubles have just begun.

My Father is listening to every word I say,
as I tell the enemy, "Stay out of my way!"

The Sword of Truth's my battle cry:
as I use His Word, demons fly!

It's cut through chains, that's bound me for years.
and with them I've been released from my fears!

God's joy has been released into my spirit,
to the point that I can hardly contain it!

"The victory is mine!" I begin to declare,
"Jesus has overcome, there's no need to fear!"

When my Jesus gave His life on the cross,
He recovered everything that was lost!

So, when fatigue from life's battles have come,
I'm reminded of what Jesus has done!

4. NEW LIFE IN JESUS

Jesus' death on the cross, that day gave everyone the opportunity to have a personal relationship with Him and eternal life. This is only possible if we choose to believe in and follow Him.

Jesus conquered the sting of death, by giving the opportunity of eternal life. It is our choice and ours alone.

God's love shows through the cruelness of the crucifixion of His only Son, Jesus. Who else do you know, who would do that to show their love for another? There is no one that can.

But God demonstrates His own love toward us, in that while we were still sinners, Christ died for us.

Romans 5:8

New Life in Jesus

O the joy that floods my soul,
when Jesus cleansed and made me whole!

He took away my sin and strife
and gave me His eternal life.

The life that flows from deep within,
that only Jesus gave, from Him.

God, the Father, Jesus the Son,
Holy Spirit three in one.

His name is Jesus and He'll never change,
the devil was conquered at his own game!

The game that gave Jesus the power,
to overcome all sin in every hour.

His love portrayed upon the cross,
that was displayed at great cost.

A cost I could never repay,
but He still loves me anyway.

His love that flows so freely within,
to those who will give their lives to Him.

This new life that only Jesus can give,
will overflow to others, from within.

5. HIS GRACE IS SUFFICIENT

Because of the Cross, our lives can be changed forever! It's so easy to fall into the enemy's trap of deception. With all that's going on in the world today, God is reaching out with His message of the Cross. Showing that our situation often needs His grace.

Imagining God giving His unmerited grace, through the death and resurrection of His Son is unfathomable to our finite minds. What we need to understand is God's Grace is sufficient for everyone!

> *And He said to me, "My grace is sufficient for you, for My strength is made perfect in weakness." Therefore most gladly I will rather boast in my infirmities, that the power of Christ may rest upon me.*
>
> **II Corinthians 12:9**

His Grace is Sufficient

This world we live in is so full of strife,
it's hard to imagine our lives without Christ.

When will this world take a breath and finally see,
that Your grace is more than *enough* to be free.

Free from all this world has to offer,
Free from sin and all the scoffers.

Thinking the costly Cross would be *enough*,
as it depicts the love You have for us!

The enemy's lies have creeped in,
into the hearts of women and men.

Filling their hearts with strife and despair,
causing their hearts to no longer care.

It's no wonder the world's like this today.
So many hearts have been hurt, in so many ways.

The "lights" of this world, need to shine brighter,
eliminating everything that sin has to offer.

With the power contained in One crucifixion,
comes His Holy Spirit, to bring spiritual conviction.

6. HIS DIVINE LOVE & PEACE

The world that we live in today is full of various "storms" of strife. There is only One who can speak peace to them: Jesus Christ, God's only begotten Son.

We may think, at times, that society holds many of the answers we're looking for, but there is only One person who can get to the "root" of all our troubles. Jesus. No one else on Earth can tell you which path is better for you to walk on. Only the Holy Spirit can enable you to have discernment for that path. Once we are on the right path, love and peace will flow like a river within us. Then and only then, will we begin to experience a sweet release, as we surrender all our anxiety and burdens to God. Experience *His Divine Love & Peace* today, won't you?

> *A man who has friends*
> *must himself be*
> *friendly, But there is a*
> *friend who sticks closer*
> *than a brother.*

> ### *Proverbs 18:24*

His Divine Love & Peace

There are so many thoughts turning in my mind,
but Jesus' love and peace are always on time.

His love is overflowing my soul,
keeping my emotions in control.

The Father's love - it is so great,
He sent Jesus to take our place.

Jesus, you're my only peace,
You lift me up when I am weak.

This love and peace that's joined together,
is constantly making all things better.

Resting in the Lord above,
is the best thing I have done.

When you're in need of a friend,
He'll stay with you till the end.

He's One that is closer than a brother.
Turn to Jesus, He's like no other!

PART SIX: SPIRITUAL WARFARE

*You are of God, little children, and
have overcome them, because He
who is in you is greater than he
who is in the world.*

I John 4:4

Figure 6: White Mountain Range

In the book of John, chapter 16, verse 33, Jesus says, '. . .In the world you will have tribulation; but be of good cheer, I have overcome the world.' This scripture is just one of many examples of what the believer's life is, daily, but as His Word states, "I have overcome the world." We, in turn, cannot be 'overcomers' until we have submitted our lives to the Lord.

In other words, Jesus knows what your life is like, and He wants you to have a perception of each trial, through His eyes. Once we surrender our lives to Him, our eyes can now see exactly to what He is seeing. Whether it be compassion, grace, mercy, peace, etc.

1. THE VICTORIOUS BATTLE

When we put on the whole *Armor of God*, our chances of winning spiritual battles, becomes so much greater! Every morning we can choose to put on our *armor* or not.

When we take the time to acknowledge God's Word, we're taking ahold of the *Sword of the Spirit*. The *Helmet of Salvation* shows forth our allegiance to God's Army. Strapping our feet with the *Gospel of Peace* in preparation for the attacks of the enemy, the *Shield of Faith* protects us from the fiery arrows of the enemy. The *Belt of Truth* must be fit to our waists in such a way that our personal integrity and moral courage reflects who we are in Christ. When our *Breastplate of Righteousness* is worn, it shows forth our *upright heart*. Are you wearing God's Armor today?

So, the king of Israel answered and said, "Tell him, Let not the one who puts on his armor boast like the one who takes it off.

I Kings 20:11

The Victorious Battle

I've declared to the enemy he will not win!
He's lost this battle because I will not give in!

The battle that's raging within my soul,
has gradually begun to take its toll!

The ones I love most are being victimized,
within this battle taking place in my mind.

The harder I pray, the worse it becomes,
even though I know the battle's been won.

For Jesus, with His death on the cross,
He arose, overcoming at all costs!

Now He holds the keys to death, hell, and the grave
and we too can arise in His mighty name!

So, you see, we can live each day in harmony,
with the very One, Jesus who has set us free!

Daily praising His name you'll soon see,
it's just the start of your destiny!

2. PRESS ON!

When God created us, He intended each of us to be a part of His Kingdom. There's still a lot of people in this world that don't want to believe in what they can't see with their eyes. Once we become a part of the Kingdom, we are encouraged to persevere, through all our circumstances that change daily. None of us are perfect and we won't be till we go to be with Jesus. So, keep your chin up and keep pressing on!

> Not that I have already attained,
> or am already perfected; but I
> press on, that I may lay hold of
> that for which Christ Jesus has
> also laid hold of me.
>
> ### *Philippians 3:12*

Press On!

When my day has started wrong,
I find myself, not so strong.

As exhaustion takes its toll,
I must press on towards the goal!

Although my body refuses,
my spirit will never lose it.

For what's mine is Yours and what's Yours is mine,
this will never change till the end of time.

Jesus Christ, He is my Lord and Savior.
Dwelling in Him, my faith will not waiver.

When that final day has come, I will shout,
"Jesus is alive beyond any doubt!"

3. JESUS CARES

This poem was written after I had gone through a depressing period in my life. Yes, even Christians feel depression and, like sheep, tend to go astray. Being depressed sucks the very life out of you if you let it! That's why it's so important to keep our eyes on Jesus.

When you are feeling down and feel you can't go another step further – Call out the name of Jesus! Say His name repeatedly! There is power in the name of Jesus! Upon doing so, you will immediately feel the difference in your spirit. I realized that in the quietness of just saying His name, He does care! As you begin to read this poem, I hope it comforts you as much as it did me.

And Jesus, when He came out, saw a great multitude and was moved with compassion for them, because they were like sheep not having a shepherd. So He began to teach them many things

Mark 6:34

Jesus Cares

I am left with a memory of my past,
just to know that Jesus loves me, at last.

Feeling oh, so much despair,
but I am told. . .*Jesus cares.*

Emotions continue to go up and down,
for I feel like, in my sorrows, I'll soon drown.

I then begin to think of hopeful things
and begin to cut off all sinful strings.

The Holy Spirit then awakens me,
that my Heavenly Father has set me free!

4. NO FEAR LIVES HERE!

When I first heard about *Covid-19*, immediately the Holy Spirit spoke to my heart saying, "This will be a *stretching* time for the whole world, especially for believers!

The biggest thing that hit me, was the *fear* of the "unknown."

As believers, we shouldn't allow the enemy to sabotage everything that the Lord has given us, yet some of us do. The believers in every part of this country should "buckle up" and know that God will be there from the beginning to the end of everything we go through. Romans 8:31 (NKJV) says: ... *If God is for us, who can be against us?* We need to boldly, with confidence, use our Armor (Ephesians 6:11-18) that He gave us to use, knowing we can be victorious!

> *For God didn't give us a spirit of fear, but of power, love and self-control.*
>
> **2 Timothy 1:7 (AMP)**

No Fear Lives Here!

Fear, you've no place in my life,
there's already enough strife!

My Lord, God and Savior, Jesus Christ,
has come to free me this very night.

All the strongholds I may have,
I freely place in His hands.

He has crushed all of Satan's schemes,
replacing each with Christ-like themes.

Peace will be replacing all my fears,
for Jesus, my Lord, is always near.

Others may doubt Him, in all of His ways,
but I say to you, His Words will not fade!

His Words convict the hardest of souls,
so that they can be brought into the fold.

Peace and love will always reign together,
but fear has no place here whatsoever!

Please hear me, all my sisters and brothers,
let's be wise when we speak to each other.

We need to show the world how we should be,
when we're united, in God, we are free!

PART SEVEN: MOURNING

Trust in the Lord with all your heart,
And lean not on your own
understanding;

Proverbs 3:5

Figure 7: A Sunrise

As believers, we know where we will be going, when we leave this life. We're only passing through. There is no reason to fear death either! When a loved one leaves this life, if they know the Lord, we know they will be seen again one day. It still feels like a piece of our heart's missing. Our Heavenly Father always has His shoulder ready to cry on and a listening ear, as well. He knows what it's like to lose someone close and dear to our hearts.

You see, the saying "time heals all wounds" can only have its *true* effect if you have Christ in your life. Some people are still waiting for that *time,* only to reopen those wounds.

Christ is the only one who can heal your wound, no matter how deep and hurtful it may be. The very heart of Jesus is moved with compassion for you, because of His love for you.

You *can* and *will* get through your time of grief.

1. JOY COMES IN THE MOURNING

The inspiration of this poem originally began when I heard of a dear friend's dog that had died. My friend was brokenhearted over the loss of her beloved *family member*. I wanted to give her a big hug and be there to comfort her, but we were miles away from each other.

This poem came from my heart and with the Lord's help, *Joy Comes in the Mourning*, came to be. She requested that I read it to her before mailing it to her. The original writing had a picture of a dog that looked exactly like hers. She loved it, framed it, and it now hangs on her bedroom wall.

> *...I will turn their mourning to joy, Will comfort them, And make them rejoice rather than sorrow.*
>
> **Jeremiah 31: 13**

Joy Comes in the Mourning

When someone dear to us leaves this life,
it causes us to be sad and cry.

Our hearts are aching at their loss,
as we lay them before the cross.

Yet we'll still think about memories we've shared,
knowing that one day we'll also be there.

Although we're mourning and will miss them dearly,
it still seems like we'll forever be weary.

Joy will return with shared memories in our hearts,
for we know we'll see them when we depart.

Away from this temporary place,
where we will see Jesus face-to-face.

2. HIS GUIDING LIGHT

We are called to be a light to those who don't know Jesus. Oftentimes though, we need to be reminded that God will give us the tools to get through each trial that comes our way. No matter how *dark* it may seem in our lives, Christ will always be there to guide us.

Just as God provided for the children of Israel, He will provide for us also. He provided them with a *pillar of fire by night* for 40 years. We need to start thanking Him and praising Him for blessings He has already bestowed on us!

> *Then Jesus spoke to them again, saying, "I am the light of the world. He who follows me shall not walk in darkness but have the light of life."*
>
> ***John 8:12***

His Guiding Light

When things aren't going as well as I'd like,
my Father comes in with His wondrous light.

His light always draws me closer to Him
and while in His embrace, it never dims.

The arms of my Father are gently strong,
as long as I'm with Him nothing goes wrong.

He's with me in each step I take,
even in my darkest of days.

His light shines upon me, and I will never stray.
Its warmth will forever guide me each and every day.

PART EIGHT: SALVATION

I am the door. If anyone enters by Me, he will be saved, and will go in and out and find pasture.

John 10:9

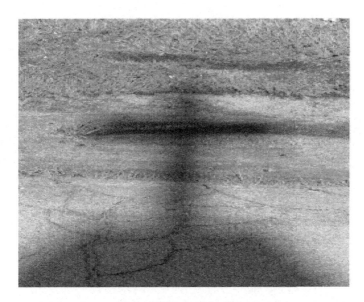

Figure 8: Shadow of a Cross

Jesus knew the pain He would have to suffer, but He was still completely surrendered to the will of God. He literally laid down his life, not only *at* the cross, but *on* the cross for us! He gave His human life for us, by showing His *Sacrificial Love* that would cover the sins of the entire history of mankind. Jesus' death and resurrection was the highest price that was given to redeem us back to God *Heart Sight* shows that the world would have us believe our sin is too big or deep for God to forgive, but that is so far from the truth! In the poem, *The Sacrificial Lamb*, from the time of Jesus' birth, Jesus took our place on the cross for the forgiveness of our sins, no matter how big or how deep they are!

He was *The Priceless Gift* that was paid for all mankind. Past, present, and future sins of each one of us, born and to be born on earth, were forgiven! All we must do is confess that we are sinners and believe in Him. Seems simple, huh? It is, but you need to make a commitment and for some that's not so easy. In the poem, *resurrected to be Born Again,* we can see what His believer's goals were. Among them, to reign with Jesus, for all eternity!

Just as we see in *The Invitation*, He has given us a choice:

to continue doing things our way, or to realize how much
we need a Savior. You've heard the expression, 'there is light at the end of the tunnel'? Jesus *is that* light! Begin to follow Him today, won't you? It's the most important decision you'll ever make.

1. HIS SACRIFICIAL LOVE

Only one person could give His life as a *blood sacrifice* to cover all our sins. Past, present and future! Giving Jesus as the ultimate sacrifice, was a unique way for God to show His love towards us. Without God's Son, we would not have the opportunity to have a relationship with God, the Father. We have nothing to lose, for we'll one day reign with them!

> For to me, to live is
> Christ, and die is gain.
>
> ***Philippians. 1:21***

Heart Sight

The heart of the world is so blind,
it only sees what is behind.

As believers we need to see,
what was clearly meant to be.

No time to stop and think,
don't watch the world as it sinks!

Lost souls falling prey to their sin,
the kind that burrows deep within.

Lord, please hold us closer to You,
that we will see the things You do!

Guide us to the place of Your rest,
after we have gone through the test.

The test of Your sweet love, oh so true,
which opens our eyes to behold only You.

Fill our hearts with more of You each day,
so, we're not blind when You come our way.

Many are blind to what lies within,
The greatest fate of their own sin.

Even with our eyes wide open,

oftentimes we're always hoping.

Hoping for a better "someday",
when You'll come and take us away.

Oftentimes our eyes can't see,
because our hearts are not set free.

3. THE SACRIFICIAL LAMB

To lay down His own life, in total surrender to God's will, Jesus became the ultimate sacrifice for all. What made this sacrifice so special is that it revealed the very heart of the Father. His unconditional love for us. Before the beginning of time God planned the birth, crucifixion and resurrection of the *Lamb*, Jesus Christ, His *only begotten Son.*

Our heavenly Father knew Jesus was the only way to re-establish His relationship with mankind. That relationship had been broken when Adam and Eve sinned in the garden.

With Jesus' last breath, the veil was torn from top to bottom. It was known to all believers that God (symbolizing the top of the veil) was opening the way for us to come in and fellowship with Him, one-on-one (no priest required). That truly was a victorious day!

The next day John saw Jesus coming toward him, and said, "Behold! The Lamb of God who takes away the sin of the world!

John 1:29

The Sacrificial Lamb

Born of a virgin,
sent for one purpose.

To give His own life,
leaving all else behind.

His ministry grew, as the Father willed,
yet there would be others rejecting Him still.

His body stretched out and nailed to a cross
those dear to Him, thought all had been lost.

With Jesus' last breath He declared, "It is finished!"
and those that remained saw that Jesus meant it!

This man, who had claimed He was the Son of God,
moved them to believe, He was truly The One!

Upon the third day,
He came up from the grave.

God's only Son became the Savior for all,
and paid a great price, for which He was called.

The spotless Lamb for all to see,
was ultimately sent to set us free.

Do you know this Savior I'm speaking of?
He is God's Son, whom I truly love!

Our Father's love for all of mankind,
had been on His heart before there was time.

Jesus' sole purpose was to give us a choice,
to worship Him fully or reject His voice.

So, what will you decide today?
Will you give Him your heart or just walk away?

4. THE PRICELESS GIFT

Jesus came as a man, yet He was still God's Son. He gave His life as a cleansing sacrifice for all. No other person in the history of mankind, ever displayed such a miraculous act of God's love! It's His heart's desire to walk with us daily.

Jesus surrendered Himself, in obedience to the Father. God has presented Himself to all of us, through the Son. He tells us in His Word, that we are all created in His image. Will you receive this *priceless gift*, from the very heart of our creator?

> *So God created man "in His" own image, "in" the "image" and likeness of God He "created" him; male and female He "created" them.*
>
> **Genesis 1:27**
> **(Paraphrased)**

The Priceless Gift

How can I doubt His never-ending love for me,
when He died and rose again, just to set me free?

His blood has the power to cleanse the darkest souls
and willingly claims them back, young and old.

Jesus, the price You paid that day,
still remains *priceless*, so they say.

You gave all You had on Golgotha's cross,
to redeem us no matter what it cost.

The most beautiful gift sent from above,
One oh so priceless, God's very own Son!

5. RESURRECTED TO BE BORN AGAIN

This world is filled with all sorts of people, from different walks of life. Once we are reborn into God's Kingdom, we begin to understand that God has the final word before He allows anything to happen to us. Whether it be life or death.

Without Jesus, we cannot survive, spiritually. Jesus makes that truly clear in the Bible. We don't always understand His direction for our lives, but we can know that we can *trust* Him with our lives.

The world we live in has drifted so far from God's ways. Until it repents and realizes God is still in control and has been the entire time, it will be apart from Him for eternity.

Jesus came to this earth, as God in the flesh. He gave His life on the cross and rose three days later. Our *resurrection* was made possible when we were *born again* into the Kingdom of God. Jesus gave His life for our salvation, allowing us to have a one-on-one relationship with the Living God!

Therefore, if anyone is in Christ,
he is a new creation; old things
have passed away; behold, all
things have become new.

2 Corinthians 5:17

Resurrected to be Born Again

Though I may be surrounded by negativity,
my Heavenly Father is always guiding me.

Sometimes I don't understand,
how He does His master plan.

One thing I know for sure,
He is the only cure.

Within this antidote is Jesus' blood,
empowered by God's purifying love.

Poured out for all the world to see,
it claims our lives eternally.

Yes, forever we will be freed from sin,
with our resurrected *Savior – born again*!

6. THE INVITATION

We often think we know what's best for our lives, but there's only one person that can make our *journey* through life bearable. He gave His life for us, in obedience to God's will, so that we could have a personal relationship with the Father. He loves us that much!

He is waiting for you today. Nothing else in this world, can give you the peace that only Jesus can give, joy instead of sadness, and a *knowing,* in your heart, that you were created in His image, and you have a purpose and a destiny in life! Give Jesus a try, won't you?

> *Behold, I stand at the door and knock.*
> *If anyone hears My voice and opens the*
> *door, I will come into him and dine with*
> *him, and he with Me.*
>
> **Revelation 3:20**

The Invitation

I'm traveling through this world, but never alone.
Someone is always with me wherever I go.

My walk with Him is rooted in faith, hope and trust,
but most of all, in His unconditional love.

His peace surpasses all my understanding,
for He's my Savior, Mentor, and Friend everlasting.

His name is Jesus. You can know Him, too.
Right now, He's waiting; He's waiting for you.

Please don't hesitate; don't put it off!
If you do wait, your soul could be lost.

He knows your heart's been broken in so many ways.
Only Jesus can mend it; please let Him today.

So, come to Him; come to Him; come to Him now!
You never know when His trumpet will sound!

PART NINE: ARE YOU READY?

In My Father's house are many mansions...I go to prepare a place for you. And . . . I will come again and receive you to Myself...

John 14:2-3

Figure 9: Sun Through the Clouds

In *A Reflection of the Father's Heart,* we see a view of God's heart, expressing His love for us through His Son, Jesus. The Heavenly Father poured His entire being into His Son and literally gave all He had to redeem us back to Him.

Jesus was and still is, *God's Master Design.* God doesn't waste anything, and He predestines each of us to specific callings in our lives. Jesus knew what His mission was here on earth, and that was to fulfill the Father's will and not His own. Jesus' sole purpose was to redeem the human race. God's creation. God's children. Jesus accepted *The Perfect Assignment,* pleasing in the sight of God. We can't imagine the pain that Jesus bore for us! He persevered, despite the battle that lay ahead. Raised from the dead, *He Rose* reveals that people were looking for a Savior. In their eyes, a hero!

The Battle Within, shows that a battle still rages in our daily lives. We are reminded of the blessings we have attained and of the trials we've gone through. It breaks His heart to see our lives hindered by the comforts of this world. Not all are willing to yield to the Lord Jesus: those who do, are looking forward to His second coming.

Those who refuse to listen are blinded to the fact that Jesus is the long-awaited *Messiah*. He isn't just the image of God, but God in the flesh. The great I AM, Himself! Even though Jesus was fully human, nothing could keep Him from submitting to the will of the Father. This was despite the pain He would have to endure fulfilling God's plan and accomplishing His entire goal in life.

Just imagine the questions we will have in our minds when we see Him. We'll have a lot of questions, right? How many of those questions will vanish when Jesus makes eye contact with us? This personal relationship with Him can only happen if we: 1) realize we are sinners; 2) believe that Jesus died on the cross to redeem us from our sins; and 3) make the decision to repent (turn away) from that sin. In this way, we become His followers. Are you ready to make this decision? I assure you it will be the most important decision you have ever made in your life!

1. A REFLECTION OF THE FATHER'S HEART

The very heart of God could be seen through the birth of Jesus Christ. Jesus became the only man that could take on the all the sins of the world. No one else could have gone through such a cruel, but necessary deed.

God used Jesus to show the love He has for each of us, and to open the door to a personal, one-on-one relationship with our Savior. The Word of God explicitly says that if we seek the Lord, we *will* find Him.

We, as His creation are a reflection of the Father's heart, as well. What is His heart showing you right now?

> *But from there you will seek*
> *the Lord your God, and you*
> *will find Him if you seek Him*
> *with all your heart and with*
> *all your soul.*

Deuteronomy 4:29

A Reflection of the Father's Heart

He gave of His heart so we could be free,
in His presence for all eternity.

This same One came to earth,
born of a virgin's birth.

A special day for all indeed,
people came, the child to see.

He would be a stranger to many,
while others that followed were aplenty.

God's heart was shown through Jesus, His Son.
Many were blind to Him as *The One.*

Jesus had done the will of the Father,
even though His life here would be over.

It seemed so final that dark mournful day,
when they came and took His body away.

Away to His temporary home,
and even this tomb was not His own.

Three days later He arose as He said
when those all around Him thought He was dead.

Soon word had spread of His resurrection,

and with this event they saw His perfection!

Oh, what a glorious day it will be
when Jesus' face we finally see!

Other's will see their unbelief was wrong,
drawing them into the believer's throng.

God's heart reflected on *Golgotha's Cross*,
came to redeem all of the lost.

2. GOD'S MASTER DESIGN

God brought Jesus into the world as a babe, but He was perfect in every way. He was first known as *Immanuel,* meaning "*God with Us.*" This holy babe, in a manger, was an extension of our Heavenly Father's unconditional love for us.

Jesus gave up His life on the cruel Cross, but He rose in victory! This was God's ultimate gift He gave to us so that we could be victorious in our own lives, as well.

All we must do to receive this gift is to recognize we are sinners, believe in our hearts that Jesus is the Son of God, believe that He came to die on the cross for us and rose again the third day so that we could be saved. Yes, it's that simple. Believe and receive!

> *Until now you have asked nothing in my name. Ask, and you will receive, that your joy may be full.*
>
> **John 16:24**

God's Master Design

Of all the things God has created,
nothing He's made has ever been wasted.

His ultimate work for the whole world to see,
as it is displayed in each living thing.

His supreme design came from above,
Immanuel, God's beloved Son.

Tenderly displaying His glorious birth,
three wise men came to acknowledge His worth.

With God guiding His steps here on earth,
Jesus soon saw how many were hurt.

Being filled with more compassion each day,
knowing there'd be hard times coming His way.

His life soon fulfilled the Father's mission,
as their handiwork fulfilled His wishes.

God's redemptive plan would be complete,
His master design would soon be seen.

Although Jesus had died on the cross,
not one piece of God's work was lost.

Making our lives matter even more,
with Jesus' life He evened the score!

3. THE PERFECT ASSIGNMENT

God's compassion for His creation was shown through our Lord and Savior, Jesus Christ. When Jesus was born, He had a divine assignment: To redeem mankind from their sins, by taking our place. This opened the door, so that we could have a relationship and live with our Heavenly Father for eternity.

Jesus had to go through changing circumstances in His life, just as we do, to accomplish His mission. He knows the pain that we endure daily -- emotional, physical, and mental. He even suffered and died on a grueling cross.

Any time we're given an *assignment* to complete, we normally are inclined to focus on the task one day at a time. Some days are harder than others. When we don't visualize the result in our minds, each day becomes harder and harder to accomplish. That's why Jesus was able to submit to the will of the Father like He did. He knew that apart from the Father He could not possibly do anything in His life. That's the way it is with us. We can't do anything without Jesus. He saw the result and with His last breath, He said, "It is finished!" He was the *Perfect Lamb* of God fulfilling the mission He was born for. The *Perfect Assignment.*

We each have a destiny i.e., assignment for our lives. We may not know what that is yet and that's ok. He will show us as we begin to seek Him first (Matt. 6:33). As we are molded and shaped to prepare for the purpose God has for us, we will be able to see the destiny He has in mind. He's always there with us in whatever circumstances we are going through. He wants to walk with us *through* the fire! He will *guide* us through it, if we let Him.

> *So, when Jesus had received the sour wine, He said, "It is finished!" And bowing His head, He gave up His spirit.*
> **John 19:30**

The Perfect Assignment

Destined to redeem all sinners from strife,
this was the assignment for His life.

As His true mission began to unfold,
they couldn't see He was the One foretold.

Human, with feelings, like all of us,
but still focused on God, with His trust.

He became the sole sacrifice,
willingly giving up His life.

Soon to fulfill His mission foretold,
the enemy predictably failed to be bold.

Jesus Christ achieved His *True* mission,
so, we too must live in submission.

Jesus, showing full compliance that day,
when those cruel guards came and took Him away.

Knowing soon it would all be over,
He looked up and over His shoulder.

"It is finished!", Jesus said while on the cross,
His mother and disciples felt the great loss.

Rising three days after that vile execution,
He revealed to the world the extent of His mission.

Breaking forth in a glorious way,

He's done the hard part,

and gave from His heart.

From His death and resurrection,

what have we learned of His connection?

The Father's compassion, shown on the cross,

was for our freedom, not for our loss.

You see the *True Mission* in life always will be,

to tell others how they too can truly be free.

A life that's free from all worry and strife.

Will you make that your main mission in life?

4. HE ROSE

Jesus resurrected on the third day, as He said He would. It was known that areas within our hearts needed to be repented of. All-in-all, God's love was ultimately expressed through His Son, Jesus. Had Jesus only died, God's plan would have remained incomplete (no personal relationship could have happened). Completed in the resurrection, a "paid-in-full" stamp was placed upon each of our lives. God's love expressed through His only Son, Jesus. Wow, what a price His Son paid for you and me! Christ's resurrection settled the final cost of our sin, once and for all.

If Jesus had not risen from the dead, we would not have the choice to have an open and established relationship with the Trinity. He desires to reveal His heart to us daily, but that can only happen if we submit our will to Him.

Jesus said to him, I am the way, the truth, and the life. No one comes to the Father except through Me.

John 14:6

He Rose

If ever there were a hero in my life,
it would be someone who could wipe out all strife.

Heroes have been known for saving lives,
but only One gives eternal life.

Every hero that's been part of tradition,
has been hindered from completing their mission.

The only hero that will forever reign,
has been living in my heart, even today.

The Father, Son, and the Holy Ghost,
they are the heroes I love the most.

The Heavenly Father, Creator of all,
sent this "unknown" Hero to redeem "the fall."

The "fall" of man because of Adam and Eve,
led to God's heroic plan to set us free.

Jesus, God's Son, was sent to die for all of mankind,
which was a heroic plan put in place before time.

A sacrificial heroism given for us,
a beautiful display of God's everlasting love.

There've been many heroes that have come our way,
but only Jesus conquered death on the third day.

You can put your trust in Him today, if you choose,
for this is One Hero who will stay true to you!

5. THE BATTLE WITHIN

It's so easy to be swayed by the beliefs of this world unless we are first rooted in Jesus. Our *spiritual roots,* in Jesus, will run even deeper as our trust in Him grows. This can only happen as we exercise our faith, by believing in Him.

As we become more yielded to our Savior, we will be able to see His hand in each conflict encounter. He is fighting with us and for us! Jesus said in His Word, that we should be of good cheer, because He has already conquered all our battles for us! The whole purpose of each battle we go through, is to reveal and strengthen our weakest points in our spiritual walk with the Lord.

> *For whatever is born of God*
> *(the believer) overcomes the*
> *world. And this is the victory*
> *that has overcome the world –*
> *our faith.*
>
> ### *I John 5:4*
> ### *(paraphrased)*

The Battle Within

While pond 'ring a thought, I had today. . .
How blessed we are in so many ways.

Yet we seem to complain about this and that,
always wondering why, we have such a task.

Secure with things that can hinder our walk,
directed away from the persona of God.

How it must sadden His loving heart
when we choose *not* to live out our part.

We, as believers, long for the day
when Jesus comes to take us away!

Sadly, not all will go to be with the One.
Rejecting Him, they've chosen to die undone.

6. TEARS FLOWING WITH ANSWERS

When we meet Jesus face-to-face, we can be sure that we'll have a list of questions to ask Him. As we gaze into His eyes, we will see what's in *His* heart. Our list begins to diminish, as we see the truth that dwells within Him. His peace envelops our hearts, as we listen to His. All our anxieties and fears become a thing of the past as we draw nearer to Him.

Our tears that had once built a wall around our heart, are now breaking walls down, in Jesus' name. Our tears have answered all the questions that we ever had, for our Lord and Savior. Revealing a once hidden wall, we can now rest in His arms. All the things of this world are not important to us anymore and they are now a part of our past. Completely submitted to Jesus, we have established a trust from our heart to His. This can only be done if we listen to Him.

The sacrifices of God are a broken spirit, A broken and a contrite heart –These, O God, You will not despise.

Psalm 51:17

Tears Flowing with Answers

When His eyes have met with mine,
several questions come to mind.

Questions of many uncertainties,
as His gentle Spirit speaks to me.

Removing all my fears and doubts,
all these questions quickly fade out.

Questions I've had for so many years,
are now being melted by my tears.

Tears that have always covered my heart,
causing my spirit to break apart.

All derived from my lack of listening,
when the Lord's Spirit, I was quenching.

Questions only He would ask.
All of them kept in my past.

"Gath' ring up all My believers," He'd say,
"You need to take care of your past today!"

Have I done as He has asked?
Taken care of my ugly past?

I must submit to Him all my fears,
including everything held so dear.

Will you prayerfully ask this question, too?
How much of your walk, in Him, is still true?

We should all be preparing our hearts for our groom,
as some of us need to be making more room.

The questions that have haunted us for years,
will be washed away with all of our tears.

PART TEN: PRAYERS

Rejoice always, pray without ceasing, in everything give thanks; for this is the will of God in Christ Jesus for you.

I Thessalonians 5:16 - 18

Figure 10: Pelican prayers

These prayers are written from different aspects of my life. Each one was inspired by different loved ones that are facing strenuous circumstances. Some are broken, others are in mourning, interceding for a grandchild, or caring for a loved one. We are called to come before God, the Father, believing He will answer our prayers, and becoming servants for the Lord, by honoring Him in everything we do or say to one another.

Beginning with *The Prayer for the Brokenhearted*, it reflects not just a broken heart, but a broken spirit, as well. In *The Mourner's Prayer*, we move from brokenness to mourning. Our lives (even the lives of our pets) are known to God who knows everything the future holds. From mourning to the heart of a grandmother, *The Prayer of a Grandmother's Heart*, shows the love she has for her grandson. Looking into *The Prayer of a Troubled Soul*, we realize, as believers in Christ, we too have our "down" times. Every day is a spiritual battle, a whirlwind of emotion that floods our souls. As time seems to stand still, the enemy tells you lies, seeking to destroy your joy, but Jesus is always there in each battle we face. *The Caregiver's Prayer* talks of how frustrating things can be when taking care of someone. Whether it be a loved one or someone else, it can be challenging and very exhausting (mentally and physically) at times.

Relying on the holy spirit's strength instead of our own becomes vital as we exercise our hearts to glorify Him.

The next prayer is *The Believer's Prayer*. Surrendering our lives to Jesus should be happening daily. Just to know we can talk to Him, anytime and anywhere, is awesome! He's a friend who "is closer than a brother". He's a friend who is available 24/7! In this prayer, we are reminded that "His strength is made perfect in our weaknesses".

The Servant's Prayer is where we ask the Lord to accept our daily sacrifice as a "sweet fragrance." This prayer asks us to think before we open our mouths to speak, knowing He will always be by our side, through the good times and bad. Thank you, Lord, for helping us through our lives.

1. THE PRAYER FOR THE BROKENHEARTED

This prayer was written after I had heard of the brokenness of a mourning mother. This mother's heart had been broken by her son's unexpected death. She felt so alone. Her brokenness brought her to her knees, but it wasn't out of respect for God. She was angry!

Her response to words of comfort were, "I don't know who or what I have faith in anymore!"

When the grieving woman's mother and I had first talked, she told me of the effects that her grandson's death had on her daughter's whole being (body, mind, and spirit). Listening to her mother, the Lord caused my heart to break for her daughter. God's heart blessed and spoke this prayer into existence. I pray for the daughter, to this very day.

Have you lost someone close, in your life? God can lift that heavy burden from your shoulders. He loves you so much!

The Lord is close to the brokenhearted and saves those who are crushed in spirit

Psalm 34:18 (NIV)

The Prayer for the Brokenhearted

Lord, I truly love You with all of my heart!
Help my loved ones, as they're falling apart.

Help them grasp the true meaning of Your words,
as it gratifies their spiritual thirst.

Your words of peace, hope and love,
that only come from above.

They're hurting so much; their hearts are so broken.
Renew their strength, with Words You've spoken.

Their beliefs are quickly fading,
their souls need resuscitating.

Your Word has promised we can trust You.
In this, Lord, give them joy anew.

The enemy is torturing them inside and out,
but Your Words are more powerful, without a doubt!

Sharper than any two-edged sword,
removing the pain from the soul's core. *

We'll see them joyful and whole once more,
as Your relationship with them is restored.

Being thankful as we meet,

as I lay them at Your feet.

I pray Your love will shine on through,
as they're reaching out for You.

Once they're able to stand on their feet,
they will reign with vic 'try, not defeat!

*Hebrews 4:12

2. THE MOURNER'S PRAYER

This prayer was written concerning a friend who had recently lost her husband. Even though his time was limited, he lived each day as it was given to him.

We don't know when our last day on earth will be. Our last breath. Our last heartbeat. Oftentimes, when we are mourning someone's death, we like to think of the potential *legend* that they left behind. What will we miss about that person the most? Most likely we'll remember the good that they did for others and the good times we shared with them.

We don't understand why some of our loved ones are taken, particularly if they are young and innocent. One moment they're full of life and then, in an instant, they're gone. Even though we realize they've gone to be with the Lord, it still leaves a void in our hearts.

He heals the brokenhearted
And binds up their wounds
[healing their pain and
comforting their sorrow].

Psalm 147:3 (AMP)

The Mourner's Prayer

I don't always comprehend what You've planned,
but I know Your love is more than I have.

You comfort me in times of dismay,
when my tears have washed all words away.

Leaving my life at the foot of the cross,
I submit it in exchange for all of the costs.

Each day is guided by Your light,
so, I may see You through the night.

My heart often leads me to sorrow,
but each day brings a new tomorrow.

Lord, I lift my hands up to You,
giving You everything I do.

Oh, how my heart is breaking,
while other's hearts are aching.

Although I don't understand,
I know they're with You at last!

3. THE PRAYER OF A GRANDMOTHER'S HEART

I wrote this, while sitting with my grandson in the emergency room. This was his first encounter with the ER, since he had started exhibiting visible signs of emotional distress.

As a grandmother, my heart was breaking for this child. Not only had we raised him and taken care of him, but I was the closest friend he could have at this moment. Being with him through "thick and thin," I felt more responsible now than ever. While he was asleep, this prayer began to pour out of my heart.

Do we realize how valuable we are to the Lord? Our worth, to our Heavenly Father is priceless in His sight. Can we imagine, for a moment, God bringing us to where we are today? Jesus is in heaven interceding for us, every second of every day. That means, at this very moment, he is praying for us. No matter what our circumstances are, He is our closest friend.

My little children, these things I write to you, so that you may not sin. And if anyone sins, we have an Advocate with the Father, Jesus Christ the righteous.

1 John 2:1

The Prayer of a Grandmother's Heart

Oh, dearest grandchild of mine,

why is your heart so blind?

Before you were formed,

God knew you'd be born.

Having a purpose for your new life,

knowing much of it would be strife.

He gave you a destiny,

that you will later see.

We are beginning to perceive,

God's destiny is now within your reach.

With your heart growing stronger to do His will,

He's working through you, as you need Him still.

God's loving care,

brings you through despair.

One day you'll tell of His great love for all,

and how for Him nothing is too great or small.

You'll be able to speak through the pain,

knowing there's much to be gained.

I know in my mind,

it will be in God's time.

4. THE PRAYER OF A TROUBLED SOUL

This poem relates to a depressed child of God. They feel so alone, but still very aware that the Lord is by their side. *He will never leave us or forsake us!*

The enemy is always trying to find ways to get us to doubt God's love for us and what He can do for us. At times it seems depression never stops. Tears often seem to wash our faces of all the joy, love, and peace that Jesus has promised us.

When we're feeling downtrodden, look to Jesus. Repeat His name verbally, repeatedly. Jesus, Jesus, Jesus, Jesus! There *is* power in His name! The power in His name will wipe away all thoughts of worthlessness and any other doubtful thinking. It will only work if you believe, though. Do you trust Him to stand you up amid your circumstances?

> *Let your conduct be without*
> *covetousness; be content with such*
> *things as you have. For He Himself has*
> *said, "I will never leave you or forsake*
> *you."*

Hebrews 13:5

The Prayer of a Troubled Soul

I have no one to talk to, but you Lord,
so, would You appear to me in True form?

A quake of emotions is smothering my soul,
as my body begins to shake, out of control.

Tears pour in my spirit like rain,
as it continues to happen again and again.

My loved ones are going away
and they seem more distant each day.

My mouth speaks before thinking,
then I feel my heart sinking!

I try so hard to be as I think I should be and
my family feels there's something wrong with me.

The harder I try the more my tears flow.
Lord, won't You repair the hole in my soul?

Replace my weaknesses with Your great strength.
Knowing You'll do this increases my faith.

My faith in You grows even stronger,
as I'm holding on even longer.

The longer I cling, the better I'll get.
The eternal war is not over yet!

5. THE CAREGIVER'S PRAYER

Being that this prayer was written on a more personal note, I understand how frustrating it can be. Needing the Lord's strength is of the utmost importance on a day–by–day basis.

In some cultures, the elderly is not only respected in the home, but are taken care of when "at home" care is needed. Long term care facilities are avoided at all costs, because the at home care is given by the surrounding family.

It's a comfortable asset to have family take care of their loved ones, when it comes to that time in their lives. We often tend to rely on our own strength to accomplish this consuming task, instead of the Lord's strength. His strength needs to be depended on, especially when we have other *little ones* to care for.

Instead of the children learning how to care for themselves, it becomes the elderly no longer able to care for themselves. They become more dependent on you, the family member.

Despite our daily circumstances, plus our patience being tried, the need for dependence on Jesus becomes more evident. Jesus said we are overcomers, because *He has overcome the world (John 16:33 NKJV).* To be an overcomer though, we must depend on His powerful strength and not our own. We will wear ourselves out, caring for the elderly, without His help!

I can do all things through
Christ who strengthens me.

Philippians 4:13

138

The Caregiver's Prayer

Lord please give me the strength to be more like you!
It seems I'm stumbling on everything I do.

The loved one I care for pushes me over the edge.
I'm suppressing my thoughts that want to be said.

In the middle of my soul's turmoil,
I can feel my blood begin to boil.

You overcame the world with Your resurrection,
That powerful Word changed my direction.

6. THE BELIEVER'S PRAYER

All of us will have days that don't go as smoothly as expected. During those troublesome times, the enemy will bring doubts into our minds, causing us to question our own salvation! This is when we need to lean on Jesus the most, for our strength.

Surrendering all our cares to Him is the only way we'll make it through any circumstances in our lives. Once we begin to act on this, our spiritual eyes are opened to visualize just a picture of how much God really loves each of us.

The closer our walk is with the Lord, the more we begin to sense His presence, while He's walking us through each segment of our lives. Sweet peace, that only Jesus can give, will be there to embrace us at the end of each day.

But those who wait on the Lord shall renew their strength; They shall mount up with wings like eagles, They shall run and not be weary, They shall walk and not faint.

Isaiah 40:31

The Believer's Prayer

Lord, please be with me throughout the day,
as things have not been going my way.

Fill me with Your Spirit Lord,
like You've never done before!

Help me not to lose faith in You,
as doubts grow in all that I do.

Use my weaknesses unto Your glory,
as my life is lived out in each story.

I surrender all that I have to You,
and every given breath I've used.

Used to move closer to You Lord,
as I'm learning to love You more.

May I feel Your hand holding mine,
as I walk through this life in Your time.

The day is now ending as I go to sleep,
resting in the arms of my Savior's sweet peace.

7. THE SERVANT'S PRAYER

As believers, we are servants of the Lord. The Lord inspired me to write this prayer when a family from church felt the Lord leading them to move to another location in Texas. Joe would be taking a position overseeing one of the sister churches.

They were so obedient to follow the Lord's leading! This was not a small family either, so you can only imagine the mixed emotions that took place. Nevertheless, the children had already begun to see God's hand in the "big move." One of the children had an answer to prayer already waiting for her upon their arrival! I saw how the children were growing spiritually, without them even realizing it.

We need to be obedient like that! It doesn't mean we will always move, but our spiritual growth moves forward as we're obedient to His callings. As *servants* of the Most High God, we need to submit our lives to Him daily.

> '...*Assuredly, I say to you,*
> *inasmuch as you did it to one of*
> *the least of these My brethren,*
> *you did it to Me.'*
>
> **Matthew 25:40**

The Servant's Prayer

Let my ways, in all I do,
be a sweet fragrance to You.

Lord, help me to see before I speak,
to be strong and not be weak.

Help me to be a servant true,
and live my life solely for You.

While on my journey through this life,
give me the strength to endure strife.

Strife that happens through each day,
as you're showing me the way.

All my steps are ordered by You, Lord,
knowing You'll be with me in Your Word.

My prayer I will now conclude,
in thanks for all that You do.

Despite my ups and downs,
You've always flipped my frown.

I love You Lord with all my heart.
Please hold me tight and never depart.

NOTES/THOUGHTS

About the Author

Linda Delgado grew up in Springfield, Missouri and later moved, with her family, to the great state of Texas! Soon after that, she graduated in 1977.

It was never in her plans to even think about writing, much less poetry. God had other plans for her though.

As her relationship with the Heavenly Father grew, so did her love for His son, Jesus Christ. She began to share what the Lord would put on her heart, at first on Facebook. Each post was entitled *Matters from the Heart (*with a heart at the end).

Soon after that, poetry started springing forth. Each poem had a story to tell. Some were inspired by loved ones and others just from the heart. During this time, *Living Poems: From the Father's Heart*, began to take shape. Just going on what is inspired by the Lord, every poem came to be and has blessed several people, while in the making.

Her cousin, Mike Goins, felt there should be other Living Poems in the future. "Maybe, maybe not," she would always reply.

We never know what God has planned for our lives, but one thing is for sure – God wants to be (and should be) glorified in everything we do!

Made in the USA
Middletown, DE
05 November 2022

13938173R00089